Network Marketing Survival 2

"Choose The Right Company, Plan, Team And Marketing Model And Explode Your Business Today!"

from the Library of the
New Thrive Learning Institute

Get Related Materials

from Our Free Library

Instant Access – Join Here

Click or type into your browser:

http://livesensical.com/go/byob/

LEGAL NOTICE

Table of Contents

Chapter 1: Introduction

Welcome To "Network Marketing Survival 2"

In this book, you will learn about everything you need to know about how to survive in the cut-throat world network marketing and how you can get ahead of the competition in the 21st century!

After all, network marketing is like a jungle. If you are not careful, you will get eaten by the LIONS out there!

If you've read the first book – "Network Marketing Survival", you will know how much different the network marketing industry has evolved since the 50s.

Of course, there are certain timeless principles that will never change in the network marketing industry. Principles such as:

> 1. Providing value for your customers and prospects
>
> 2. Uplines helping downlines (and sidelines helping one another)
>
> 3. Working together with a solid management team
>
> 4. Building your reputation and helping others...

These things will never change. However, there are certain things like business opportunity demands, prospecting methods, competition and many other crucial business factors have changed the way network marketing is done!

The goal of this book is to provide awareness for network marketers and give them enough knowledge to know what works and what doesn't work. With this knowledge, you will be able to arm your downlines to the teeth!

Make sure you apply the techniques in this book and take advantage of the free tools that are available for you. Just reading this book is not enough. You have to take action and make your business a part of you; otherwise you will not be able to achieve success.

Chapter 2: Network Marketing In The 21st Century

Sales Versus Marketing

Times have changed since network marketing was introduced to the world. We must be very careful how we approach our prospects, however.

Just because the profitability of network marketing is still viable doesn't mean that using the same old techniques that are used in the 80s is not going to get you the same results in the 21st century!

Here is the irony part – when the term 'network marketing' was coined, everyone focuses on the first word rather than the second. In other words, they go around networking instead of marketing!

Most people who are in network marketing do not have a CLUE what marketing is all about! They go about recruiting friends and family on their name list while deluding themselves into thinking that they are 'sharing' or 'marketing' their products to people.

MYTH: Network marketers are not in sales, they are merely sharing products with other people

TRUTH: Network marketers who do not have a marketing system in place are actually in SALES.

What they are actually doing is that they are SELLING an idea to someone else. Whether they are selling the product or the opportunity, they are trying to convince someone to change their mind about what they have to offer.

Remember – Sharing is different from selling. It is totally different. If you are my friend and you are having a conversation with me right now, I would share with you about my passion for eating exotic food.

When I'm sharing with you, I've no intention to SELL you exotic food (unless I am getting commissions the restaurant that cooks exotic food).

Get the idea? Selling is different from sharing.

So the question is: How do I generate business without 'SELLING'?

I'm not saying that you do not sell any products. But what I'm saying is that the approach when it comes to marketing versus selling is totally different!

Take a doctor for example.

A doctor sells his or her services. But they don't go around recruiting patients or sending out flyers and advertisements saying that they are the best gynecologist in town!

When people go to the doctor, they seek the doctor's EXPERT advice. They listen intensively to every word they have to say and they will take whatever medicine they recommend. (So much different compared to network marketing recruitment, don't you think?)

The same principle applies to marketing!

Marketers sell products, but not in the way sales people do. A person who markets their business effectively is a LEADER. They are EXPERTS. They don't go around peddling their wares like a sleazy salesman. They are good at marketing themselves in such a way that they will always:

1. Find the right target market

2. Find the right people to join their downline (and their downlines will listen to them and do what they say)

3. NOT waste their time on the wrong people

4. Attract the right people to them.

Old School Versus The Google Revolution

There was a time in the past where people have NOT heard of network marketing. If you bring them to a 'dog and pony show' telling them about how network marketing will give them residual income and CHANGE THEIR LIFE, they will gaze in awe about this fantastic NEW opportunity.

Unfortunately, network marketing is totally different today! Times have changed and network marketing is nothing new.

Network Marketing Survival #2 - 6

An average person is approached by network marketing companies at least 10 times. I personally have been approached by network marketing reps and opportunities once every month!

The fact of the matter is, network marketing is opportunities are like the sand at the beach. There are more and more companies springing up like mushrooms after the rain and the COMPANY : DISTRIBUTOR ratio is going to shift dramatically. In other words, competition is going to kill the average network marketer as a result of the Google revolution.

Today, someone can go online and Google the search term – Network Marketing Opportunity or Home Based Business and get bombarded by countless business opportunities... and they can do it in the comfort of their own home without having to drive out to Star Bucks and listen to a stranger as they 'show the plan'.

The funny thing is a lot of network marketers do not realize that the Internet has revolutionized the way that network marketing is done!

Some people are sucking in paid leads like a vacuum cleaner and earning massive money online while the poor network marketing rep who are still making a name list of friends and family and going to be crushed by the competition!

Now that we know about the competition that we are up against, you have a better understanding on how to use the Internet to work FOR YOU rather than against you!

For more information about how to use the Internet to generate leads and grow your business, click here to learn more.

Attrition Rates Are Increasing

People who drop out of network marketing companies are quite common today. However, because of increasing awareness about network marketing recruitment 'tricks', information overload and saturation, more and more people will be dropping out of network marketing companies!

In the past, people are more concerned about supporting their upline and being loyal to their company. Today, there are so many business opportunities available out there that people are jumping from one opportunity to another in a heartbeat!

They don't want to wait 6-12 months before they break even (or get their first commission check like some people do). They want fast, relevant results – just like what Google offers!

Being aware of the rising attrition rates will give a network marketer a realistic expectation about the industry rather than jumping in believing that motivation and hope will provide the ingredients for success in network marketing.

Chapter 3: Choosing The Right Network Marketing Company

The Right Vehicle

Let's be brutally honest with ourselves here.

Network marketing is all about making MONEY.

You are NOT in charity. If you are building this business because of your loyalty to your company (because you feel that it is a good company) or because you are loyal to your upline, you will FAIL IN NETWORK MARKETING IF YOUR INTENTION IS NOT VERY CLEAR FROM THE START!

A network marketing company (or network marketing for that matter) is just a vehicle for you to make money, full stop.

As an independent distributor, you are an entrepreneur! An entrepreneur must deal with partners, workers and suppliers. You are NOT in business alone (if you are, then you are not an entrepreneur but a small business person). As an entrepreneur, your network marketing company is your PARTNER.

Your business will survive if your partners are performing well. In business, people will break partnerships if it isn't profitable! The same should apply in your network marketing business as well!

Remember, your company is only a vehicle. If the management team is stuffing up, the margins are low (and not profitable), and the other variables do not equate to a profitable business, then it's better to find another company!

Remember this golden rule: Mixing business with emotions is a recipe for disaster!

The Right Management Team

The management team is the backbone of your business. They are your suppliers and your collection agents all in one. How can you survive in the network marketing industry if your suppliers are not delivering the goods on time or the company has cash flow problems?

In order to choose the right company with the right management team, you must do your due diligence on these factors:

1. Their track record. Is the network marketing company backed by a solid track record?

2. Is the team here to stay? There are some network company owners who build and burn and build again. You don't want to invested interest in a company that is there today but gone tomorrow!

3. The vision. Does the company have a solid vision and are they actively working towards that vision?

4. The capacity to expand. Sometimes, when a new startup company is expanding, they might run into cash flow problems when their sales volume increases! They need to build more warehouses, deal with shipment and pay MORE commissions and bank loans when more and more orders are taken. Just because the teams are growing and the sales are coming in doesn't mean the company is able to cope.

A Product That Is In Demand

This is a no-brainer. No matter how good your company, management team, compensation plan or your upline is, a company will NOT survive if their product does not stand the test of time.

For example, multivitamin supplements were a growing trend during the 80s. Because of the rising health needs due to pollution and people spending more and more hours in the office, it created a need.

But that doesn't mean that the trend is still growing. There are some companies which came up with supplements that do not require water for mixing or swallowing. It caters to those people who are always on the run.

Today, people are not just developing new products... they are engineering new product lines and creating new demands while diminishing existing ones. The question remains... does the demand for your product justify your efforts for promoting it?

The Right Trend

This chart below will tell you what stage you are at. Of course, there is no right or wrong as to when is the right time to join a network marketing company, because it is up to you to work out YOUR own growth.

Front Loading Companies

What is front loading?

Front loading is a bad way to build your business by 'buying rank' when you invest in an inordinately large amount of products – especially when you are just starting your business.

A lot of network marketing companies usually collapse due to unethical front loading practices disguised as a 'shortcut' to entice reps to invest more money.

If you find yourself investing in more stocks than you need for personal consumption and your monthly personal sales, then you might get yourselves into cash flow problems.

WARNING: AVOID FRONT LOADING COMPANIES AT ALL COSTS!

Chapter 4: Finding The Right People To Work Together With

Supportive Uplines And Sidelines

Are your uplines supportive people? There are people who will be there for you through thick and thin. There are even sidelines that are willing to do the same for you and your network.

Having these people on your team will definitely grow your business and the ability to leverage on them is very important.

Here is one thing that will help you to understand whether the team you are joining will work out to your advantage or not...

Let's say you have an excellent networking tool that you can use for prospecting online. Does your upline support you using it or does he or she restricts you to 'following the system' given by the company?

You be the judge of whether this will work for you or against you.

Speedy Support

Network marketing companies with poor support will get in your way of success.

You see, there are company support staff that are willing to assist you when the products are faulty. It will affect your network even if they are downline because somewhere down the line, someone's income will be affected if they are not good at handling a situation (like a faulty product or filling in the registration form).

There are some companies that even construct an online prospecting system that will help a new rep to get up to speed. But if the new downline does not know how to utilize it, it will affect him and his sponsor because they are not maximizing the system to recruit more effectively!

If your company has a solid or speedy support team, you will be able to leverage on their support! Otherwise, you will need to manually coach your downlines on how to deal with administrative work!

Joining Networking Groups Outside

Life exists outside network marketing groups. One of the best ways to touch base with other people and get more fresh leads is to join other network marketing groups such a business networks or Rotary clubs.

Even your church or religious organizations are great places to meet new people (but make sure your intention is sincere because God is 'watching').

One of the biggest problems with some network marketing reps is that some of them know NOTHING but network marketing (and network marketing jargon) to the point that they do not know how to relate to the outside world!

If you join networks such as those mentioned above, you will be able to relate to people in the 'real world' and you will be able to connect with them and expand your networks!

Chapter 5: Differentiating Between Compensation Plans

The Importance of Compensation Plans

There are many types of compensation plans out there. Some of them are so complex that it requires a degree in mathematics to figure out how much money you will get in your next commission check!

Some people tend to neglect compensation plans. They feel that it is not important at the initial stages. But if you are not very clear how to 'place' your downlines, you will LOSE A LOT OF INCOME and in some cases, some of your downlines will lose vested interest if you fail to place the right people under them.

Remember, losing 10% may not seem like a big amount but when you calculate in the long run, your sales volume could total up to THE THOUSANDS and it is even worse when it is not YOUR income because if you cause your downline to lose money due to poor planning then you will lose the trust in your leadership which is something money can't buy back!

Single Level Versus Multi-Level

What are the fundamental differences between single level marketing and multi-level marketing? Well for starters, it is more than the amount of tiers which commissions are paid.

Allow me to elaborate how the mechanics affect a person's vested interest.

Single level programs – prevalent amongst the majority of the world's pay scheme where it involves a merchant paying an affiliate or sales person, is more beneficial for the merchant (or in the network marketing scenario, more beneficial to the sponsor).

Multi-level programs on the other hand, pay many levels of marketers. In some cases, the person who personally sponsors someone and gets a sale from him, only gets a small percentage because a lot of the commission goes to his upline(s).

So how does this apply to network marketing survival?

1. Certain network marketing compensation plans usually pay more commission to those who personally sponsor someone. If their downline sponsors someone, the upline gets a lot less money. On the other hand, certain plans pay MORE to someone who builds their group (in essence, volume generated by one's downline – this ensures that the sponsor will not leave their downline without any help) It is important to recognize at which level you are getting the bulk of your money!

2. There are many programs OUTSIDE the network marketing company that that promotes supplementary

material to assist the network building process. These programs are usually SINGLE LEVEL programs that provide a secondary income to the main business. Why this is very important to recognize is because these tools are helpful for prospecting and providing cash flow that more and more marketers are using it. Single level supplementary programs are also viable because a network marketing company do not allow the rep to build more than one multi-level program at the same time.

3. Single level programs allow the affiliate to make money for THEMSELVES ONLY. You see, if an affiliate recruits another affiliate for single level programs, the 'sponsor' does not get any money as a result of his 'downline's' sale. In other words, recruiting an affiliate only creates ANOTHER competitor! This is different for multi-level programs because the affiliate can take a cut from another affiliate so that vested interest is still there. As a matter of fact, some network marketing companies even pay only a SINGLE level for the initial entry level sale of any new rep that is sponsored, so do NOT simply give away your sponsored downlines to the people in your group... you can lose a lot of money that way!

In the next sub-chapter, we will explore a number of popular network marketing compensation plans.

You do not need to have an in-depth analysis but at least understand how the structure works so that you can maximize your network marketing groups.

Unilevel Plans

Unilevel plans are one of the oldest compensation plan structures in the world and their calculation is very straight forward. Basically you are able to sponsor as many people as you can and you can draw commissions up to a certain level. In other words – unlimited width, limited depth.

A person in a Unilevel plan should focus on building as many team leaders as possible. Sponsor up to 4 to 5 people and focus on helping them build their groups (rather than building FOR them). After all, there are only 5 days in a week, helping one at a time is enough to keep one's hands full. Don't build too wide to the point that you can't help your people and they are left all alone.

Stairstep Plans

The concept is similar to the Unilevel structure but the payment and building structure is a bit different. Basically you focus building your 'rank' by climbing the Stairstep ladder of success. You usually achieve this creating or helping your downline to create sales volume.

Once you achieve a certain rank, you can override

commissions up to infinity levels.

Just like the Unilevel plan, you must focus on creating leaders in your FRONTLINE – those that you directly sponsor. Because it is worthless to have a large width of frontline when they are not producing anything.

Binary Plans

Binary plans and building structures are usually more complex because you are only allowed to have a width of 2 and place the people you sponsor under your downlines. In other words – 2 width, unlimited depth.

In a binary plan, you often have to balance both dies of your groups by ensuring that the volume produced on the left group is almost the same as the right group. Placements of downline must always work towards balancing and you have to think not only about yourself, but for your downline as well.

The Australian Two-Up

Australian Two-up plans are a bit more complex but here is a simple explanation. The FIRST TWO sales of your FRONTLINE (B) go directly to you as illustrated in the diagram on the left. But on the third (C) and subsequent sales, it goes to B.

However, the sales from the first two and their subsequent

twos (as illustrated in the B1 group will always pass up two sales up back to A and NOT B) For your reference, the color of the sales will belong to the corresponding colors illustrated above (e.g. B1, B3, B4 and B5 will go to A and C1, C2, C3, C4, C5 and C6 will pass up to B)

Practically speaking, this marketing plan should be built THIS way and no other way:

Because you need to give up two people to your upline, you must make sure you leave your STRONGEST downlines to your upline.

People make the mistake by giving the weakest to their uplines because what they don't realize is that if they drop out from the system, you will most probably not be able to draw commissions from your other groups because they require the first two to 'activate'.

Network marketing is all about duplication – so you must teach the right culture in your group by giving the two strongest downlines to your upline and duplicate it so that everyone will building a very solid network.

Matrix Plans

Matrix plans are often even more complex than the other plans above but basically you will need to fill a number of UNITS in a matrix cycle (consisting of a fixed width and depth – in the case above, it is a 2 by 2 matrix).

When a matrix is 'filled', you will be given a new account that you can use to build a new matrix and earn more money.

Most matrix plans that I've seen usually turn up on illegal scams or High Yield Investment Programs (HYIP) or other shady programs. If the Matrix plans are too complex and it doesn't facilitate building a viable downline system, you need to consider building a business that is more long term.

Chapter 6: Prospecting Methods

Here are a couple of prospecting methods that you must be aware of if you want to survive in the network marketing jungle... after all having effective prospecting methods is your network marketing lifeline!

Cold Calling & Invitations

Cold calling (and going door-to-door) is one of the MOST INEFFECTIVE and DIFFICULT form of obsolete prospecting method in the 21st century. Some sales people might debate that this is still viable, but let's be realistic...

1. YOU don't like to receive phone calls

2. Cold calling has a lot of resistance and people turn their ears away if you are a stranger

3. People don't like being sold things that they don't need

4. They don't even need to see YOU – a total stranger!

Invitations on the other hand might still work if it is done correctly. You can invite your friends to an event or a tea-party but make sure that your INTENTION is very clear when you invite him or her. People are not stupid and they can sense your intentions if you have promised them otherwise.

In other words, don't trick them into coming to your

network marketing prospecting meeting!

Classified Advertising & Google AdWords

One important thing about advertising is to ALWAYS go for direct response advertising. Do NOT burn your money on advertising that does NOT solicit direct response and a measurable way to calculate your expenditure, leads contacting you and conversion to sales!

When you advertise your opportunity on classified advertising, make sure you have a website or a phone number that they can contact you that MUST lead the prospect to the next phase of your sales funnel.

Ad Impression Direct Response/ Lead Capture Build the relationship Pitch the right offer Close sale or Follow up until the sale is closed.

The problem with people is that they dump all sorts of advertising without leading to the second phase which is the direct response or lead capture phase. They think just because they leave a website or a phone number (like leaving name cards all over town) they will get a lot of people to sign up.

With Google AdWords, you must make sure you have a system that is designed to deal with those leads and execute the steps above.

Networking Swaps

In certain business networking circles, you are able to build a list of referrals for one another even if you are in a different line of work. There are Business networking organizations like BNI (which is one of the biggest networking organization in the world) are designed to facilitate this.

Of course, all this depends on the rapport and friendship between you and the other members.

Remember that must refer business to those other members and not just sit there and wait for people to give you leads.

Online Prospecting

There are many ways you can acquire prospects online without spending money on Google AdWords.

You can drop by people's blogs, go to forums or build a mailing list of prospects in order to build relationships and meet new people.

Social networking sites like MySpace, Friendster, Facebook, MyBlogLog and many other web 2.0 sites are a great place to meet new people with similar interests and make friends with them.

You must be very careful of one thing, NEVER, NEVER EVER SPAM forums, blog comments or other people's email. It is a very quick way to get a bad reputation or banned from those forums.

Chapter 7: Developing The Posture Of A Leader

Posture Is Everything

One of the most important aspects of surviving in the network marketing world is to develop the ALPHA mentality in your business. This is very important because nobody remembers who came in SECOND!

It is human nature to look towards a leader and if you are not the leader of your organization, you are most likely following someone else's direction and you are not in charge of your business.

Bring a leader in network marketing requires you to prospect effectively. After all, you want to position yourself as an EXPERT and not as a PEDDLER!

Read this line very carefully:

Nobody who bought a drill actually wanted a drill.

They wanted a hole.

Therefore, if you want to sell drills, you should ADVERTISE information about making holes – NOT information about drills! – Perry Marshall

Remember, it is pointless to sell someone something they don't want and appear like a sleazy salesman in the process.

Ways To Develop The Winning Posture

Here are a few tips on how to develop the winning Posture:

1. Dress sharply and ALWAYS be natural

2. Don't treat everyone around you as your prospect – the last thing you want to do is to appear desperate for their money

3. EDUCATE people on the viability of using your product and become a living testimonial rather than pushing the products in their face

4. Diversify your prospecting methods by going online

5. Invest in your education about the Network marketing Industry.

6. Invest in prospecting tools that you can use to leverage your business with!

Chapter 8: Conclusion

Network marketing is quite a challenging industry but the most important thing you must do is never to forget that you are the captain of your ship when things go wrong. If you wound up with a bad company, find a better one and MOVE on. Don't harp on the past.

Once you are certain you are back in the game, you must invest in a winning system and learn to take your business to the next level by using the right prospecting techniques and following the right team.

Here's a brief recap on the things you MUST pay attention to when choosing the right company:

1. Be aware of the changes in network marketing during the 21st century.

2. Choose your network marketing company wisely and consider the factors such as the management team, the demand and the trend.

3. Find the right people to work with – work together with your uplines, downlines, sidelines and even the company staff.

4. Be aware of the types of compensation plans out there and keep an eye out for front-loading companies with sky-high promises.

5. What are the best ways to get new prospects and how to use online prospecting to expand your name list.

6. How to turn yourself into a true LEADER.

I wish you all the best in your network marketing adventures.

SEE YOU AT THE TOP!

Bonus

Get Related Materials

from Our Free Library

Instant Access – Join Here

Click or type into your browser:

http://livesensical.com/go/byob/

www.ingramcontent.com/pod-product-compliance
Lightning Source LLC
Chambersburg PA
CBHW021853170526
45157CB00006B/2434